Level 2

The Nature Kid's Guide to
WOODPECKERS

DAVID ANDERSON

LP Media Inc. Publishing
Text copyright © 2026 by LP Media Inc.
All rights reserved.

For information address LP Media Inc. Publishing,
30012 Variolite St NW, Princeton MN 55371
www.lpmedia.org

Publication Data

Woodpeckers
The Nature Kid's Guide to Woodpeckers — First edition.

Summary: "Learn all about Woodpeckers, the Nature Kid Way"
— Provided by publisher.

ISBN: 979-8-89818-164-2

[1. Woodpeckers – Non-Fiction] I. Title.

Title: The Nature Kid's Guide to Woodpeckers

CONTENTS

FOREST HOMES

Stomp, stomp, stomp! A woodpecker hops up the bark.

Knock knock knock! That sound echoing through the trees means a woodpecker is nearby. These remarkable birds show up in places most people would never expect, from dense rain forests to sun-baked deserts to snowy mountain slopes.

Wherever they live, woodpeckers have one thing in common. They need trees, especially old, dead, or dying ones. Soft rotting wood is easy to peck through, and the holes they carve make perfect sheltered homes.

Cool damp forests, dry open woodlands, hot scrubby deserts — if there is a tree worth pecking, a woodpecker has probably found it.

WHERE WOODS ARE

The yellow-bellied sapsucker **migrates**. It flies south each winter.

Tap tap tap! A woodpecker drums on bark. It looks for bugs inside.

Woodpeckers are found on nearly every continent on Earth. North America, South America, Europe, Asia, and Africa all have their own species. Only Australia and Antarctica have none at all.

Some species are famous in their home regions. Pileated woodpeckers rule the forests of North America. Great spotted woodpeckers are a common sight across Europe and Asia.

Most woodpeckers stay in the same area all year long. Home is home!

SMALL STUFF

The bar-breasted piculet is only 3 inches long. This tiny woodpecker lives in South America.

Tap tap tap! A little downy woodpecker pecks at the bark.

Woodpeckers come in a surprising range of sizes. The downy woodpecker is one of the smallest in North America, about the size of a sparrow and light enough to land on a thin weed stalk without bending it.

The pileated woodpecker is a completely different story. It stands nearly as tall as a ruler and weighs about as much as a baseball. When this bird goes to work on a tree, the chips fly far.

The great spotted woodpecker falls right in the middle, roughly the size of a robin and built like a little powerhouse.

BUILT TO DRILL

A woodpecker's tongue wraps around its skull to reach deep into tree holes!

Tap, tap, tap! A woodpecker drums against a tree trunk.

Woodpeckers have special bodies built for pecking trees. Their beaks are hard and pointed like chisels. Strong neck muscles absorb the shock of each strike — the force would knock out any other animal, but woodpeckers feel nothing.

Their skulls have special spongy bone that cushions each peck. Their brains fit tightly inside their skulls, which keeps them safe. Stiff tail feathers brace against the tree like a third leg, and two backward-pointing toes lock onto bark so they never slip while working.

SUPER SENSES

12

Listen! A Red-headed woodpecker tilts its head and hears something moving just beneath the bark.

Woodpeckers are hunting machines built from the inside out. Their hearing is so sharp they can actually detect the tiny sounds of insects moving under tree bark, even through several inches of solid wood.

Their eyes are just as impressive. Woodpeckers can spot a small insect from far away. Special eyelids snap shut a split second before each peck, protecting their eyes like safety goggles.

They even feel vibrations through their feet, sensing hidden bugs moving deep inside a tree without seeing them at all.

STAYING SAFE

Woodpeckers can spread their wings to look bigger and scare enemies.

Shhh! A woodpecker presses against the tree bark. Its colors help it blend in.

A woodpecker sitting still on a tree trunk can almost completely disappear. Their brown, black, and white feathers match bark so well that even a sharp-eyed **predator** can walk right past without noticing.

When danger arrives, woodpeckers press their stiff feathers flat against the tree and freeze. Staying perfectly still is often enough to stay safe.

But if that does not work, they start drumming. That loud, fast knocking warns other animals to back off and stay away.

BUG BUFFET

DID YOU KNOW?
Woodpeckers can eat poison ivy. It does not hurt them!

Chomp! The hungry woodpecker eats a tasty grub.

Woodpeckers love to eat bugs. Beetles, ants, and caterpillars are their favorites. Some woodpeckers eat over 900 beetle **larvae** in one day!

They also eat other foods. Many like tree sap and berries. Acorn woodpeckers store thousands of acorns in tree holes.

In winter, bugs are hard to find. Woodpeckers then eat more nuts, seeds, and fruit. Some visit bird feeders. They like suet and sunflower seeds.

PECK POWER

FUN FACT!

Some woodpeckers catch insects in midair! Others use their tongues to slurp up ants.

Tap-tap-tap! A great spotted woodpecker hammers at the tree.

A woodpecker's beak hits wood up to 20 times per second, drilling through bark that would stop almost any other animal cold.

It starts with a light tap. This helps the bird find hollow spots where insects are hiding. Then it hammers through.

Once the hole is open, the real secret weapon appears. A woodpecker's tongue can stretch up to five inches past its beak, with a sticky tip that pulls insects straight out of their tunnels.

Some woodpeckers skip the drilling entirely and simply peel bark away to find bugs crawling underneath.

WATCH OUT

DID YOU KNOW?
Woodpeckers fight back! They can jab predators with their beaks!

20

Hiss! A snake moves close to the woodpecker's tree.

Life as a woodpecker means watching out from every direction. Hawks and falcons strike from above, sometimes snatching a woodpecker right off a tree trunk. Sharp-shinned hawks are especially dangerous to smaller species.

The threat does not stop at night. Great horned owls hunt in silence and darkness, and raccoons and weasels raid nests while woodpeckers sleep.

Perhaps the sneakiest predator of all is the rat snake. Its slim body slides right into a nest hole, reaching eggs and chicks that seemed completely safe.

FLY FAST!

Woodpeckers fly in a bouncy up-and-down pattern that makes them much harder for predators to track and catch in the air!

Splash! A woodpecker zips away through the misty forest.

When danger gets close, a woodpecker's first move is speed. These birds can launch off a tree and disappear into the forest in seconds, weaving between branches in fast, bounding flight that is hard for a predator to follow.

If flying is not the answer, they think fast in other ways. A woodpecker will dart around to the other side of a tree trunk, putting solid wood between itself and the threat.

As a last resort, they press flat against the bark and go completely still, trusting their patterned feathers to do the rest.

HOP AND FLY
DID YOU KNOW?
Woodpeckers can fly up to 25 miles per hour when escaping danger!
24

Stomp! Little woodpecker feet hop along the branch, then wings flutter.

Woodpeckers move in ways no other bird quite does. Instead of walking up a tree, they hop — short powerful jumps that carry them up the trunk with surprising speed.

Their stiff tail feathers act like a kickstand, pressing against the bark to keep them steady while they work.

Their feet are built for gripping. Two toes point forward and two point backward, locking onto bark so tightly that a woodpecker can hang sideways or even upside down without slipping.

DAY FLYERS

Stretch! A woodpecker lands on a branch in the morning sun.

Woodpeckers are **diurnal**. This means they are active during the day. They wake up when the sun rises.

Mornings are busy times. Woodpeckers search for food right away. They also drum and call to mark their territory.

At night, woodpeckers rest in tree holes. They tuck their heads under their wings. Most sleep alone in these cozy homes.

Woodpeckers take short naps during the day. These naps can last from a few seconds to about 20 minutes!

SOLO STARS
FUN FACT!
Acorn woodpeckers share their home with their grown children for years!
28

Stomp! A pileated woodpecker drums alone on the old oak tree.

Most woodpeckers are solitary birds. They stake out a territory and defend it fiercely, drumming loudly to warn others that this patch of trees is taken.

During nesting season a mated pair works together. Both parents take turns keeping the eggs warm and feeding the chicks. Some woodpecker pairs bond for life.

Once the young birds leave, the quiet returns. Each adult goes back to living alone, ruling its own stretch of forest until the next spring rolls around.

DRUM DANCE
FUN FACT!
Some woodpeckers drum on metal roofs and gutters. The louder sound attracts more mates!
30

Rumble! The woodpecker beats a rhythm on the old tree.

Woodpeckers drum to attract mates. Males tap their beaks against wood up to 40 times per second. This loud sound travels up to half a mile away.

Each species has its own drumming pattern. Females listen for the best drummers.

Most woodpeckers mate in spring. Males attract females by drumming and showing off bright head feathers. After pairing, both birds build a nest hole together.

CUTE CHICKS

DID YOU KNOW?

32

Splash! Fluffy woodpecker babies wiggle in their cozy nest.

Baby woodpeckers are called chicks. They hatch from white eggs inside tree **cavities**. Most woodpecker pairs lay 3 to 5 eggs at a time.

Newborn chicks look very different from adults. They have no feathers at all. Their skin is pink and see-through. Their eyes stay closed for about 7 to 10 days, too.

Chicks are born completely helpless. They have soft beaks that harden as they grow.

PROUD PARENTS

The father usually sleeps in the nest with the chicks at night.

Chirp, chirp! A proud woodpecker parent feeds his chicks.

Both mothers and fathers feed the chicks. They bring insects and larvae to the nest many times each day. The hungry chicks beg loudly for each meal.

As the chicks grow the parents teach them how to find bugs. Young birds watch and copy what their parents do. They learn to peck at bark and probe for insects.

Chicks stay in the nest for about 4 weeks. Then they climb out and begin to fly. Parents still feed them for a few weeks. Soon the young woodpeckers live on their own.

FOREST BUILDERS

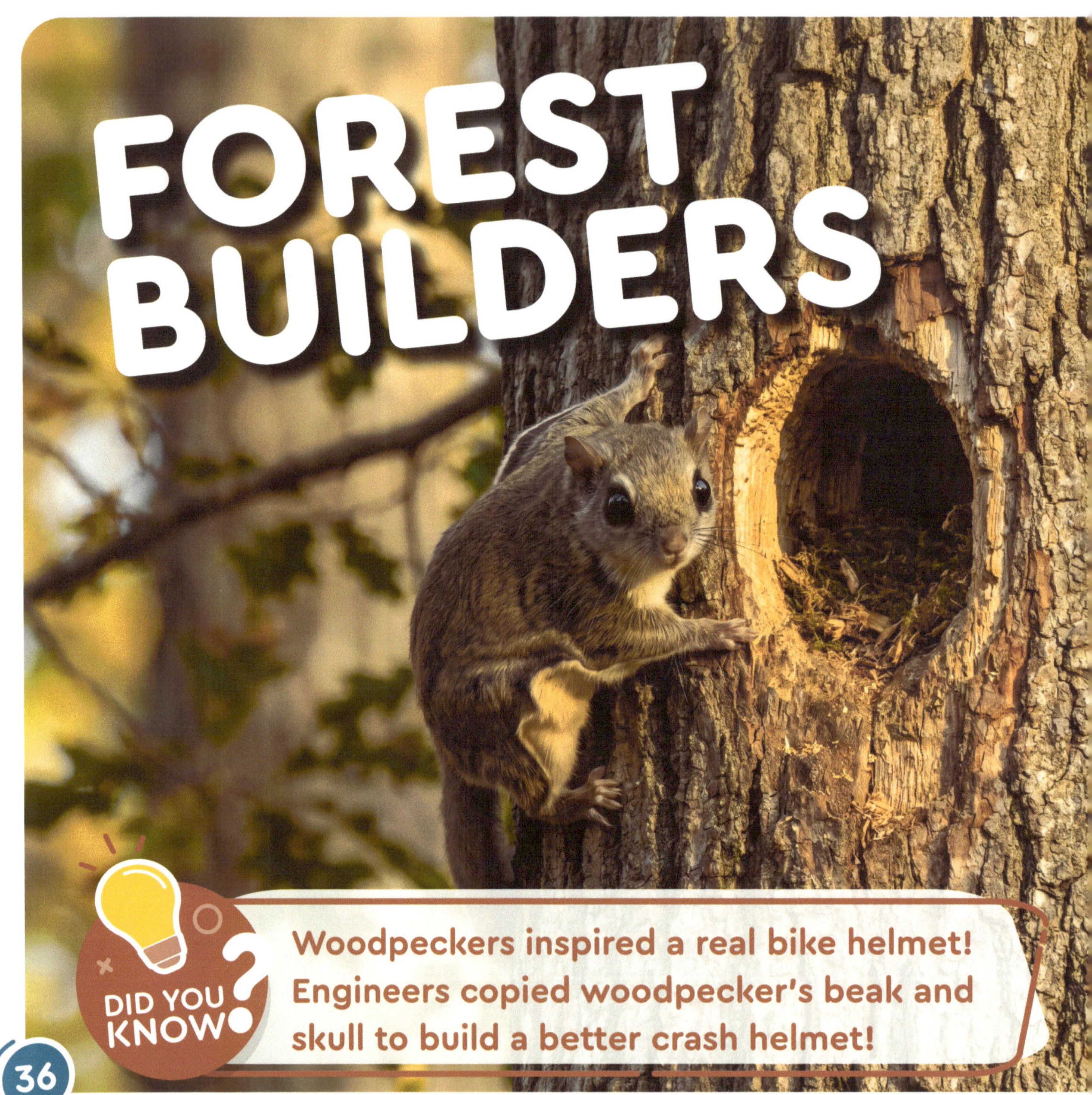

Look! A flying squirrel climbs into its hole. It did not make that home — a woodpecker did!

Woodpeckers do something most people never notice. Every hole they carve becomes a home for another animal. Owls, squirrels, ducks, and bats all rely on old woodpecker holes to raise their families. Without woodpeckers, many of them would have nowhere to go.

Scientists call this a keystone species. Take the woodpecker away and the whole forest feels it. Insects go unchecked and dozens of animals lose their homes.

SPOT ONE!
FUN FACT!
Early morning is the best time to spot woodpeckers. They are most active then!
38

Flap! A woodpecker lands on a branch at a park.

You do not need to go far to find a woodpecker. A park, a backyard, or any place with trees is a great starting point. Listen first — that drumming or tapping sound will lead you right to them.

Once you spot one, move slowly and stay quiet. Sudden movements send them flying. Binoculars help you see their colors and markings up close without getting too near.

Watch how they move up a trunk, tilt their head to listen, and work a hole. Every visit teaches you something new.

GLOSSARY

diurnal
Active during the day and sleeping at night.

migrates
Travels to a different place when the seasons change.

predators
Animals that hunt and eat other animals.

larvae
Baby insects that look like tiny worms.

cavities
Holes or empty spaces inside trees.